AF228593

CHICAGO BULLS

BY TODD KORTEMEIER

SportsZone

An Imprint of Abdo Publishing
abdobooks.com

abdobooks.com

Published by Abdo Publishing, a division of ABDO, PO Box 398166, Minneapolis, Minnesota 55439. Copyright © 2023 by Abdo Consulting Group, Inc. International copyrights reserved in all countries. No part of this book may be reproduced in any form without written permission from the publisher. SportsZone™ is a trademark and logo of Abdo Publishing.

Printed in China.
052022
092022

Cover Photo: Charles Rex Arbogast/AP Images
Interior Photos: Jeff Haynes/AFP/Getty Images, 4, 10, 37; Susan Ragan/AP Images, 7; John W. McDonough/Icon Sportswire, 8; Focus on Sport/Getty Images Sport/Getty Images, 12, 14, 26; Paul Natkin/Getty Images, 15; Bettmann/Getty Images, 18; Jonathan Daniel/ Getty Images, 21; Paul Beaty/AP Images, 23; John Swart/AP Images, 24; Beth A. Keiser/ AP Images, 28; John Swart/AP Images, 29; Jonathan Daniel/Getty Images, 33; Mark Elias/ AP Images, 34; Cliff Welch/Icon Sportswire, 38; Jack Smith/AP Images, 39; Ben Margot/AP Images, 41

Editor: Charlie Beattie
Series Designer: Joshua Olson

Library of Congress Control Number: 2021951677

Publisher's Cataloging-in-Publication Data

Names: Kortemeier, Todd, author.
Title: Chicago Bulls / by Todd Kortemeier
Description: Minneapolis, Minnesota : Abdo Publishing, 2023 | Series: Inside the NBA | Includes online resources and index.
Identifiers: ISBN 9781532198229 (lib. bdg.) | ISBN 9781098271879 (ebook)
Subjects: LCSH: Chicago Bulls (Basketball team)--Juvenile literature. | Basketball--Juvenile literature. | Professional sports--Juvenile literature. | Sports franchises--Juvenile literature.
Classification: DDC 796.32364--dc23

TABLE OF CONTENTS

ONE LAST SHOT

Time was running out in Game 6 of the 1998 National Basketball Association (NBA) Finals. The Chicago Bulls led the series 3–2, but they trailed the Utah Jazz 86–83 with 41.9 seconds remaining in the game. Thankfully for the Bulls, they had Michael Jordan, the best player on the planet.

Jordan caught an inbound pass from Scottie Pippen, then drove around Utah's Bryon Russell. Soaring to the hoop, the Bulls' star laid the ball into the basket. That gave Jordan 43 points for the game—and, more importantly, cut Utah's lead to one.

For the Bulls, more than a championship was on the line. The players knew that this series might be the end of an amazing era. Jordan and Pippen, both future Hall of Famers, led the team. They had one of the most successful coaches of

In 1998 Michael Jordan led the Chicago Bulls to their sixth NBA Finals in eight seasons.

all time in Phil Jackson. Together, the three of them had led the Bulls to five NBA titles in the last seven years.

But the players weren't getting any younger. Jordan had already come out of retirement once. Pippen was 32 years old and wanted an expensive new contract. Meanwhile, Jackson and Bulls general manager Jerry Krause weren't getting along. Jackson had already said he would not return to coach another season. And Jordan said he wouldn't play for anybody but Jackson. All signs pointed to this being the last chance at another championship for these Bulls.

The 1997–98 season had been a tough one for the Bulls. They dealt all season with the question marks surrounding their future. Pippen was injured for the first 35 games. The team started just 12–9. But Jordan was still in his prime. He would win his fifth NBA Most Valuable Player (MVP) Award for his work in the regular season. And he had help from teammates such as Toni Kukoc and Dennis Rodman, who was one of the NBA's best-ever rebounders.

The Bulls eventually shook off their slow start. At 62–20 they coasted into the playoffs. The first two playoff rounds were a breeze. Chicago went through the New Jersey Nets and Charlotte Hornets easily. But things got tough when the Bulls met the Indiana Pacers in the conference finals. Chicago won the first two games. But the Pacers, coached by NBA legend Larry Bird, won three of four to force a winner-take-all

One of Dennis Rodman's, *right,* main jobs during the 1998 NBA Finals was defending Utah's hall of fame forward Karl Malone.

seventh game. The Bulls hadn't had to play a Game 7 in four years. Jordan rose to the occasion again. He scored 28 points in an 88–83 victory to send the Bulls back to the NBA Finals against the Jazz.

The Finals were a rematch of a thrilling 1997 championship series, and again the matchup was competitive. The last two games were scheduled for Salt Lake City. Pippen had hurt his back in the conference finals. His injury flared up again after he

Bulls forward Scottie Pippen played through the pain of an injured back during Game 6 of the 1998 NBA Finals.

dunked in the first basket of Game 6. He went back and forth to the locker room for treatment all game. But he was back on the court with the game on the line.

LEGENDARY FINISH

Utah took its possession down the court. The Jazz had two future Hall of Famers of their own in point guard John Stockton and power forward Karl Malone. Stockton got the ball down low to Malone. Rodman was defending him. But suddenly, Jordan snuck in and slapped the ball away. He then brought it back up the court as the clock ticked under 20 seconds.

Jordan settled in with the ball on the left side of the court near the three-point line. He dribbled until there were less than 10 seconds to go. Russell guarded him. Finally, Jordan began his move toward the basket. But instead of driving, he pulled up quickly at the free-throw line.

Russell slipped, giving Jordan all the space he needed. The Bulls' superstar pulled up for a jump shot. Upon releasing the ball, Jordan let his right hand hang in the air as he watched the shot. It hit nothing but net as it dropped through the hoop. The Bulls had the lead with 5.2 seconds left.

"That may have been," said NBC broadcaster Bob Costas, "the last shot Michael Jordan will

Mr. Clutch

The word *clutch* describes a player who is good in the biggest situations. Few players were more clutch than Jordan. He hit 25 game-winning shots in his NBA career. Jordan hit 50 percent of the shots he attempted in the final 24 seconds of a game.

Michael Jordan releases his game-winning shot in Game 6 of the 1998 NBA Finals against the Utah Jazz.

ever take in the NBA. . . . If that's the last image of Michael Jordan, how magnificent is it?"

But before deciding his future, Jordan and the Bulls had to close out the Jazz. Utah ran a play for Stockton to shoot a three-pointer. But Bulls guard Ron Harper played tight defense. Stockton's shot clanked off the rim. Both teams scrambled for the rebound. By the time a Utah player got his hands on it, time had run out.

The Bulls flooded onto the court. Jordan put up five fingers on one hand and one finger on another. That made six championships for Jordan and the Bulls. The future of the team was uncertain. But what they had just accomplished was sure to linger in fans' memories.

Introducing the Champs

The Bulls became famous in the 1990s for their home player introductions. The tradition actually began far earlier, in 1977. The Bulls became the first team to turn out the arena lights during intros. In 1984, Chicago DJ Tommy Edwards, who was also the team's public address announcer, chose the song "Sirius" by the Alan Parsons Project to play in the background. It became the soundtrack to the Bulls' championship teams of the 1990s, even though Edwards was replaced by Ray Clay in 1990. Turning out the lights and playing music is now the standard all around the NBA.

BULLS LEARN TO RUN

The Bulls were founded on January 16, 1966. Although they were new to the city, they were definitely a Chicago team. Owner Dick Klein was a local businessman. Chicago native Johnny "Red" Kerr was chosen as the team's first head coach. Even the team's star shooting guard, Jerry Sloan, was from the southern part of Illinois.

Like many new teams, the Bulls had a losing record in their first season. However, their 33–48 record was still good enough to make the playoffs. They qualified for the postseason in two of the next three seasons as well. But Chicago had a losing record each time.

Because the team was not a true championship contender, fan interest began to wane. A crowd of just 891 fans showed up for a November 1968 game against the Seattle SuperSonics. Shortly afterward, the team traded for scorer Bob Love and

Jerry Sloan averaged 14.7 points per game over 10 seasons with the Bulls, and he later coached the team.

Head coach Dick Motta helped turn the Bulls into a consistent playoff team when he was hired in 1968.

hired a new head coach in Dick Motta. The next year, new general manager Pat Williams added small forward Chet Walker as Chicago continued to overhaul the roster.

The moves paid off. The Bulls jumped from 39 wins in 1969–70 to 51 in 1970–71. Chicago won at least 50 games in each of the next three seasons. The Bulls won their first playoff series in 1973–74. The next year they won their first division title and another playoff series.

FIRST SHOT AT GREATNESS

Chicago came close to the NBA Finals in 1975. The Bulls held a 3–2 lead over the Golden State Warriors. Game 6 was in Chicago. But the Bulls' offense dried up on their home floor. Golden State held Chicago to just 72 points. In Game 7 the Bulls let an 11-point halftime lead slip away.

Golden State won the series on its way to the NBA title. Chicago started to slide down the standings. Walker retired. Sloan struggled with injuries before retiring in 1976.

Artis Gilmore was a four-time All-Star during a six-season stretch with the Bulls between 1976 and 1982.

Motta left after the 1975–76 season as the Bulls were once again playoff outsiders.

However, some luck soon came the Bulls' way. The American Basketball Association (ABA), which had been trying to compete with the NBA, folded. Four ABA teams joined the NBA. And a special draft was held for NBA teams to select players from the ABA teams that had disbanded. The Bulls got 7-foot-2-inch center Artis Gilmore. Along with veteran guard Norm Van Lier, Gilmore led Chicago to a surprise playoff appearance. The big man turned into a star in Chicago, but the team's success did not last.

Several coaches tried, and failed, to bring Chicago back to the playoffs over the next eight years. Sloan was hired as head coach in 1979 after a stint as an assistant. He guided the team to a winning record and a playoff appearance in 1980–81. But Sloan was fired the next year after a 19–32 start. He went on to a Hall of Fame coaching career, but not in Chicago. Sloan eventually coached over 1,800 games as coach of the Utah Jazz.

STRIKING DRAFT GOLD

The history of the Bulls was altered on one afternoon in 1984. After a 27–55 record in 1983–84, the Bulls got the third pick in that summer's NBA Draft. That wasn't good enough to get the player everyone wanted—University of Houston center Hakeem Olajuwon. But many experts believed the draft included other potential stars, such as Charles Barkley, John Stockton, and a guard from the University of North Carolina named Michael Jordan.

The Bulls wanted Jordan. But they were stuck behind the Portland Trail Blazers, who owned the second pick. Chicago received a stroke of luck. Portland already had a great shooting guard in Clyde Drexler. They decided to take center Sam Bowie from the University of Kentucky.

Portland's choice became one of the all-time great draft mistakes. Bowie played 10 injury-plagued seasons in the NBA, only four of them in Portland. Jordan became one of the league's best-ever players.

The young guard changed Chicago's fortunes immediately. As the 1984–85 Rookie of the Year, he brought the Bulls back to the playoffs. His high-flying, high-scoring style transformed the team. Before Jordan, the team had been just another NBA also-ran. Now they were one of the league's hottest tickets.

However, even Jordan couldn't lift the team to playoff success in his first few seasons. The young star needed more help. The Bulls got a big boost at the 1987 draft. First, general manager Jerry Krause made a shrewd trade to acquire the draft rights to forward Scottie Pippen. Then he drafted power forward Horace Grant. Both players went a long way in turning Chicago from a playoff team to a dynasty.

One of the final pieces of the puzzle was a change at head coach. After making it to the conference finals in 1988–89, coach Doug Collins was fired. Krause promoted assistant Phil Jackson. A former NBA player and longtime coach at lower levels, Jackson was able to push the Bulls to new heights.

THREE-PEAT

Overcoming the physical Detroit Pistons was one of Chicago's main hurdles toward becoming a dynasty.

Jackson's first task was figuring out how to beat the rival Detroit Pistons. They were one of the top teams in the NBA's Eastern Conference in the 1980s. The Pistons played a punishing physical style, especially against Jordan. Games between the Pistons and Bulls were often intense. By the 1990–91 season, the Bulls had lost to Detroit in the playoffs three years in a row.

But it was a different, stronger Bulls team in 1991. Chicago swept away its longtime foes and moved on to play in its first NBA Finals. There, the Bulls finally finished the job and brought home a championship by beating the Los Angeles Lakers.

And that was only the beginning. The Bulls repeated as champions in 1992. They completed the "three-peat" in the 1993 Finals. That made them the first team to win three championships in a row since the Boston Celtics won their eighth consecutive title in 1966.

It seemed as if nothing could slow the running Bulls. Then came a bombshell. At the age of 29, with three league MVPs to his name, Jordan announced his retirement on October 6, 1993. Jordan cited a few reasons for leaving the game so soon. He had struggled with the death of his father earlier that year. He also felt he had nothing left to accomplish in basketball. And he wanted to leave the game on top, before his skills started to decline.

The Bulls had lost the centerpiece of their franchise. Pippen stepped in as the team leader while Jordan embarked on a new adventure playing professional baseball. The Bulls remained a strong team, winning only two fewer games in 1993–94 than they had the year before. But they missed Jordan's winning ways in the playoffs. That season Chicago was eliminated in the conference semis.

The Jordan Rules

The Detroit Pistons put all their energy into stopping Jordan. Their plan for him was called the "Jordan Rules." The basic idea was to not let Jordan get to the basket. They did that any way they could, even if they had to physically knock him down.

RECLAIMING THE THRONE

In March of 1995 Jordan surprised the NBA again. After nearly two years away, he announced a return to basketball. Jordan was rusty after joining the team for the final 17 regular-season games. The Bulls were eliminated in the semis again.

Before the next season, Krause made more smart moves. Grant had left the team after the 1993–94 season. Now Krause picked up Dennis Rodman to play power forward. Rodman was a controversial player who frequently fought with opponents and referees. He was known for his ever-changing hair color and big personality. But he was also one of the best rebounders in the NBA. The Bulls already had center Luc Longley, forward Toni Kukoc, and guards Ron Harper and Steve Kerr as key role players. The team was set at every position before the 1995–96 season.

The result was the best record the NBA had ever seen. The Bulls went a record 72–10 and rolled through the playoffs to another championship. Jordan returned to his MVP form. It was the beginning of another "three-peat."

Shortly after the 1997–98 season ended, rumors about the end of the Bulls dynasty started coming true. Jackson retired. Jordan followed. The Bulls opted to start over rather than try to keep their aging core together, even though they were still at the top of their game. Pippen was traded. Rodman signed with a new team.

THE BABY BULLS

The 1998–99 Bulls were almost unrecognizable from their championship years. Kukoc became the team's leading scorer, but the Bulls posted the worst winning percentage in team history. Fans still supported their Bulls, though, as the team finished first in the league in attendance.

Tyson Chandler was one of the many "Baby Bulls" brought in during the early 2000s. Most of Chicago's moves during that era did not work out.

The Bulls' efforts to build a new championship contender did not work out. The team got even worse by 2000–01, winning just 15 games. All those losses gave the Bulls high draft picks, and they did select some quality players. The team's new stars were dubbed the "Baby Bulls." Forward Elton Brand shared the Rookie of the Year award in 2000. But Brand was traded a year later for another young player in center Tyson Chandler. Many expected Chandler to develop into a star, but he did not. He was also traded, in 2006.

Krause retired in 2003. Former Bulls player John Paxson was hired in his place. Paxson helped rebuild the team through the draft with players such as guards Kirk Hinrich and Ben Gordon and forward Luol Deng. They formed a core that helped the team return to the playoffs in 2004–05.

COMING UP ROSES

The Bulls caught another draft break in 2008. Chicago's chances of getting the top pick at the draft lottery were 1.7 percent. But they won anyway. The reward was Derrick Rose. The point guard was not only a star in the making, but he was also from Chicago.

After two straight 41–41 seasons, the Bulls decided to change head coaches. Longtime NBA assistant Tom Thibodeau took over.

Thibodeau had an intense style, and it worked for the Bulls. The 2010–11 team won 62 games and made it to the conference finals for the first time since 1998. Rose was the first Bull since Jordan to be named league MVP.

The Bulls were just as good in 2011–12. But their championship hopes were dashed when Rose suffered a serious knee injury in the first playoff game. He missed not only the rest of the postseason but also all of the next year. After 10 games back in 2013–14, Rose suffered a different knee injury. He missed the rest of that season as well.

Rose was never the same player after his injuries. Fortunately, the Bulls had a good supporting cast with players

Derrick Rose helped lead the Bulls to their first period of extended success since Jordan's departure.

like center Joakim Noah and small forward Jimmy Butler. The Bulls remained a playoff team. But they never challenged for a championship again under Thibodeau.

Thibodeau was let go after the 2014–15 season. Rose was traded to the New York Knicks a year later. Butler carried the Bulls to the playoffs in 2016–17. They even took a 2–0 opening-round series lead against the Boston Celtics before eventually losing in six games. But Butler was traded after the season. The Bulls were rebuilding yet again. They would need to change course to get back to championship basketball.

CHAPTER THREE

BIG, BAD BULLS

Long before the Bulls featured Michael Jordan's one-of-a-kind skills, several other stars suited up in the team's red-and-black uniforms. Some of the first Bulls didn't do much winning. But the players and coaches on those teams gave Chicago an early basketball identity.

Johnny "Red" Kerr coached the Bulls for only their first two seasons. But that was just the beginning. After leaving the team in the late 1960s, Kerr returned to the Bulls' front office in the early 1970s. In 1975 he joined the radio broadcast team. He was the popular voice of the Bulls for more than 30 years. Kerr was honored with a statue outside the team's arena, the United Center, just before his death in 2009.

The Bulls teams Kerr coached were short on stars. But they did have guard Jerry Sloan. The "Original Bull" was known for his hard work and determination. Though the Bulls were not

Michael Jordan shows off his high-flying skills during the 1988 Slam Dunk Contest.

Bob Love averaged more than 20 points per game in six straight seasons for the Bulls after joining Chicago in 1968.

very good, fans knew Sloan was giving it his all.

Only Michael Jordan and Scottie Pippen played more minutes in a Bulls uniform than Sloan did. He was the first Chicago player to have his number retired. Sloan later returned to the team as head coach.

The name Jordan appears at the top of almost all of Chicago's team records. But Bob Love's name is not far behind in most categories. The 6-foot-8-inch forward hadn't received much playing time in the NBA before coming to the Bulls in 1968. Once he got the opportunity to start, Love turned into a top scoring threat. He was the team's all-time leading scorer until Jordan and Pippen passed him.

The collapse of the ABA in 1976 resulted in a big gain for the Bulls. The team was able to get center Artis Gilmore, who had been the 1972 ABA MVP. Gilmore was a force around the basket, using his long arms to block shots and grab rebounds. He remains the team's all-time leader in blocks. Gilmore stood an imposing 7 feet, 2 inches, but he was known as a quiet and gentle person off the court.

CONSTRUCTING A DYNASTY

Rod Thorn joined the Bulls as general manager in 1978. He brought back Sloan as a head coach. But the executive's most memorable move came in the 1984 draft.

Thorn knew exactly who he wanted with the third pick in the draft. The Bulls chose Jordan, a 6-foot-6-inch guard from North Carolina. His arrival would change the Bulls from a middling team to one of the most iconic and successful teams in the world. Jordan didn't just transform the history of the Bulls. His popularity raised the profile of the NBA around the globe. His soaring dunks and deadly shooting accuracy made him a threat to score from anywhere. Jordan was also fiercely competitive. He hated to lose and demanded excellence from all of his teammates.

Jordan is widely considered one of the greatest athletes of all time. His 30.1 points per game scoring average is the highest in NBA history. He won five MVPs and led the league in scoring 10 times.

While Jordan ushered in a new era on the court, the Bulls also received new ownership in the 1980s. One year after

Scottie Pippen skies for a dunk against the Indiana Pacers during the 1998 Eastern Conference finals.

Jordan was drafted, Chicago businessman Jerry Reinsdorf bought the team. Reinsdorf had also purchased baseball's Chicago White Sox four years earlier. He quickly became one of the NBA's most influential owners.

One of Reinsdorf's first orders of business was hiring Jerry Krause as general manager. Krause was known as a top basketball scout. His job was to surround Jordan with more talent.

Krause swung a trade on the day of the 1987 draft. The deal netted forward Scottie Pippen, who had just been drafted fifth overall by the Seattle SuperSonics. Pippen played at the University of Central Arkansas, a small school. But Krause scouted Pippen and saw a great athlete who could help the team.

Pippen turned out to be the perfect fit for the Bulls. He was a defensive force who could help get the ball back for Jordan. But Pippen could also score plenty himself and was an all-around great player. Jordan said the Bulls would not have won their championships without Pippen.

Krause hired an assistant coach named Phil Jackson in 1987. With the Bulls striving to win their first championship in 1989, Krause promoted Jackson to head coach over the popular Doug Collins. Jackson became one of the winningest coaches in NBA history. He also became

Phil Jackson's triangle offense and close relationships with his players pushed the Bulls to greatness in the 1990s.

the first coach since Red Auerbach of the Boston Celtics to win at least three titles in a row.

Just as the Bulls were chasing their first title in 1991, Krause drafted Toni Kukoc out of Croatia. Kukoc opted to continue playing in his home country for three more seasons. When the small forward finally arrived, Jordan had retired. The Bulls needed help. Kukoc made big shots and was also a strong passer. When Jordan returned, Kukoc provided a spark off the bench during the Bulls' second three-peat.

Guard Steve Kerr joined the Bulls in 1993. He had already played for three other NBA teams but had not had much success. In Chicago Kerr became a key reserve. Kerr later became a successful coach. His 2015–16 Golden State Warriors won 73 games. That broke the 1995–96 record of 72 held by the Bulls.

One of the final pieces added to the Bulls dynasty was Dennis Rodman. Rodman had a flamboyant personality, often highlighted by his brightly colored hair. Rodman was 34 when he came to Chicago in 1995, but he had plenty of game left. A ferocious rebounder, he was also willing to dive on the floor to save loose balls. Rodman played only three years with the Bulls and won a championship in all three.

STARTING OVER

As the Bulls tried to recapture their championship glory in the 2000s, many players came and went. Some never reached their potential. One player who did was Joakim Noah. The center was born in New York City and raised mostly in France. His parents were a professional tennis player and a sculpture artist. He grew up attending elite private schools. Noah spoke multiple languages and was known to quote Shakespeare in postgame interviews. But nobody questioned his talent or passion. Noah was incredibly competitive and a relentless defender. He became a fan favorite with his hard work and effort.

Noah's tough defense was an excellent fit for coach Tom Thibodeau's system. Thibodeau was known as a defensive specialist. He had an intense coaching style and was tough on the team. But he got the best out of them. Thibodeau's winning percentage ranks second only to Jackson in Bulls history.

Point guard Derrick Rose was an NBA superstar from the moment he was drafted in 2008. His quick drives to the hoop thrilled fans. That style of play earned him the 2010–11 MVP Award—the first for a Bulls player since Jordan. But the aggressive style also probably shortened his career. Rose struggled with knee problems that took away his speed and explosiveness in his later career.

In the late 2010s and early 2020s, Bulls fans could be reminded of the high-flying play of Rose by watching guard Zach LaVine. The two-time dunk contest champ came to the Bulls in 2017. He emerged as one of the top scoring threats in the NBA and gave fans a thrill every night with his spectacular offensive skills. In 2021 he earned a spot in his first All-Star Game.

Zach LaVine's flashy style wowed Chicago fans after he was acquired in a trade with the Minnesota Timberwolves in June 2017.

CHICAGO'S SHINING MOMENTS

The Bulls made the playoffs in six of their first seven seasons, but finding postseason success was tough. They lost in the first round each of those years.

The 1973–74 team was ready to end the streak. The Bulls entered the playoffs with their best-ever record, 54–28. But they faced a tough test against the Detroit Pistons in the first round.

The series went to seven games. Four of the first six were decided by fewer than five points. Game 7 was more of the same. Chet Walker scored 26 points for Chicago, while Bob Love added 24. But it was barely enough to keep the Pistons at bay. Chicago held a slim 96–94 lead with seconds to play. The Pistons had a chance to inbound, but the Bulls deflected the pass away and held on to win their first playoff series.

Michael Jordan holds up the Larry O'Brien Trophy after the Bulls defeated the Portland Trail Blazers in the 1992 NBA Finals.

JORDAN RULES

The excitement of Michael Jordan's Rookie-of-the-Year season in 1984–85 took a hit early the next year. Jordan broke his foot in October 1985. The team feared he would miss the rest of the year. But he returned in March and led the team on a playoff run. Facing the mighty Boston Celtics, Jordan exploded for a record 63 points in Game 2. The record came in a losing performance. But it was a sign that Jordan was ready to take over the NBA.

The Bulls were on the verge of another series loss in the 1989 playoffs. Chicago faced the Cleveland Cavaliers in the first round. The Bulls trailed by one with three seconds left in the fifth and final game. Jordan caught an inbounds pass and drove hard to his left. He rose into the air at the free-throw line and fired a shot over Cleveland's Craig Ehlo. The shot dropped through the hoop as the buzzer sounded. Jordan leaped in the air and pumped his fist in celebration of his second playoff series win. The game-winning shot is one of the most famous in NBA history.

It was far from Jordan's last iconic shot. Two years later in the NBA Finals, Jordan and the Bulls squared off with fellow legend Magic Johnson and the Los Angeles Lakers. Los Angeles had won four titles in the 1980s. But with one shot, Jordan signaled the start of a new NBA era.

The Bulls lost Game 1 at home. They came out in Game 2 and rolled over the visiting Lakers. Despite sitting much of the game with foul trouble, Jordan scored 33 points. In the fourth quarter, the Bulls put together a stretch of 12 straight made shots. Then Jordan did the seemingly impossible.

Jordan drives against the Los Angeles Lakers during the 1991 NBA Finals.

Catching a pass from Bulls guard Randy Livingston at the free-throw line, he drove down the middle of the lane. He had the ball in his right hand as he jumped for a layup. Jordan expected a defender to challenge him. As he rose toward the hoop, he switched the ball from his right to his left hand and laid it in. Like his game-winner two years earlier, Jordan's switch-handed layup became a signature NBA highlight for years to come. Chicago won the game 107–86. The Bulls then won the next three to capture their first title.

The Bulls were back in the Finals a year later. This time they faced the Portland Trail Blazers. Jordan came out firing in Game 1. He was never known as a great three-point shooter, but he hit a handful early. As he knocked in his fourth of the first half, the crowd grew louder. Then he hit a fifth. After he hit his sixth of the half, Chicago Stadium exploded. As he jogged back up the floor, Jordan looked at Johnson, who had retired as a player and was calling the game on TV. The Bulls guard simply shrugged and shook his head.

Jordan's six three-pointers in one half set a Finals record. He set another by scoring 35 points before halftime. The 122–89 rout spurred Chicago on to its second title in a row.

Out of Jordan's many iconic performances, Game 5 of the 1997 NBA Finals might have been his most famous. On the day of the game with the Utah Jazz, Jordan wasn't feeling well His stomach hurt, and he was feeling weak. But the Jazz had won two games in a row to even the series at 2–2. The Bulls did not want to let the title slip away. Just three hours before the game, Jordan got out of bed and headed to the arena.

Scottie Pippen helps an ailing Michael Jordan off the court late in Game 5 of the 1997 NBA Finals.

Though he was tired and achy, Jordan played over 44 minutes. He scored 38 points to lead all players. After leading the Bulls to victory, Jordan collapsed in Scottie Pippen's arms. Jordan's "Flu Game" propelled the Bulls to a six-game series victory.

CLUTCH SHOTS

Two unlikely heroes hit huge shots for Chicago during the Bulls' run of six titles in the 1990s.

The first of these shots came in 1993, as the Bulls faced the Phoenix Suns in the Finals. Chicago led the series 3–2 but trailed by two points with seconds left in Game 6. Pippen drove the lane, but the defense cut him off. He kicked the ball out to reserve guard John Paxson, who was open at the three-point line. Paxson drilled the shot with 3.9 seconds left on the clock. The 99–98 victory gave Chicago its first three-peat.

John Paxson was one of many lesser-known Bulls who hit big shots during the dynasty run. His three-pointer sealed victory in Game 6 of the 1993 NBA Finals against the Phoenix Suns.

Two days after Jordan's "Flu Game" in 1997, Chicago faced another tight Game 6. With the game tied 86–86 and 10 seconds left, Jordan found himself double-teamed by the Jazz. Looking toward the free-throw line, he spotted guard Steve Kerr wide open. Kerr took Jordan's pass and drilled a 17-foot jump shot to put Chicago ahead. The lead held up as Chicago won title number five.

BULLS ARE BACK

Entering the 2021–22 season, Chicago had not had a winning record in six seasons. But the team gave fans hope by winning its first four games of the year. That solid play hit new heights in December. On December 19, 2021, Chicago beat the Lakers 115–110. They didn't lose again for nearly a month.

On January 7, 2022, Chicago hosted the Washington Wizards. Behind 27 points from guard Zach LaVine and a near triple-double from center Nikola Vučević, Chicago won 130–122. The victory pushed Chicago's streak to nine games. It was the Bulls' longest winning streak in 11 years. The team

Bulls guard Zach LaVine slams home two of his game-high 27 points during Chicago's rout of the Washington Wizards on January 7, 2022.

left the United Center that night with a 26–10 record, best in the Eastern Conference. It looked like the Bulls were finally back again.

TIMELINE

1966

The city of Chicago is officially granted an NBA franchise on January 16. It is announced the team will be called the Bulls.

1966

The Bulls play their first game and get their first win on October 15.

1967

The Bulls finish their first season 33–48, the best record for an NBA expansion team, qualifying them for the playoffs.

1974

Head coach Dick Motta leads the Bulls to their first playoff series victory.

1984

With the third pick in the draft, the Bulls select Michael Jordan out of North Carolina.

1989

In his first MVP season, Jordan hits the game- and series-winning shot in the first round of the playoffs.

1991

After topping their longtime rival Detroit Pistons in the conference finals, the Bulls beat the Los Angeles Lakers in the NBA Finals to win their first championship.

1992

The Bulls beat the Portland Trail Blazers in six games to repeat as champions.

1993

On June 20, the Bulls win their third consecutive NBA title in a dramatic six-game series against the Phoenix Suns. In October, Jordan surprises the basketball world by abruptly announcing his retirement.

1995

Jordan comes out of retirement to rejoin the Bulls.

1996

After going 72–10 in the regular season, the Bulls beat the Seattle SuperSonics in six games to once again become NBA champions.

1997

With the help of Jordan's "Flu Game" heroics in Game 5, the Bulls beat the Utah Jazz in six games for a fifth title.

1998

Jordan hits the game-winning shot in Game 6 to win a sixth championship for the Bulls. Jordan announces his retirement after the season.

2008

The Bulls earn the number one pick in the draft and select Derrick Rose out of Memphis.

2011

Rose becomes the first Bull since Jordan to win league MVP.

2021

The Bulls acquire All-Stars Nikola Vučević and DeMar DeRozan to pair with 2021 All-Star Zach LaVine as the Bulls embark on a new rebuilding project.

FRANCHISE HISTORY
Chicago Bulls (1966–)

NBA CHAMPIONSHIPS
1991, 1992, 1993, 1996, 1997, 1998

KEY PLAYERS
Artis Gilmore (1976–82, 1987)
Michael Jordan (1984–93, 1995–98)
Toni Kukoc (1993–2000)
Zach LaVine (2017–)
Bob Love (1968–76)
Scottie Pippen (1987–98, 2003–04)
Dennis Rodman (1995–98)
Derrick Rose (2008–16)
Jerry Sloan (1966–76)

KEY COACHES
Phil Jackson (1989–98)
Johnny "Red" Kerr (1966–68)
Dick Motta (1968–76)
Tom Thibodeau (2010–15)

HOME ARENAS
International Amphitheatre (1966–67)
Chicago Stadium (1967–94)
United Center (1994–)

BABY BULLS

The Bulls are by far the youngest of Chicago's teams in the four major North American pro sports (MLB, NFL, NHL, NBA). Chicago has had the MLB's Cubs since 1876. The NFL's Bears came along in 1920, while the NHL's Blackhawks formed in 1926.

BIG HOUSE

Chicago's home, the United Center, is the largest arena in the NBA.

WINNING CULTURE

The Bulls have never lost an NBA championship series.

WHAT'S IN A NAME?

The Bulls got their name as a nod to Chicago's meatpacking industry, and owner Dick Klein wanted a short name that fit with other Chicago teams, like the Cubs and the Bears.

RECORD BROKEN

The Bulls' 72–10 record has since been surpassed by the 2015–16 Golden State Warriors, who finished 73–9. Steve Kerr, who played on the 1996 Bulls, was the head coach of the Warriors that season.

GLOSSARY

competitive
Desiring to win, or having as fair of a chance to win as one's opponents.

conference
A group of teams that make up half a sports league.

contender
A person or team that has a good chance at winning a championship.

expansion team
A new team that is added to an existing league.

folded
Went out of business.

franchise
A sports organization, including the top-level team and all minor league affiliates.

point guard
The player who directs a team's offense.

rebound
To catch the ball after a shot has been missed.

three-pointer
Any shot taken behind the three-point line.

triple-double
Accumulating 10 or more of three certain statistics in a game.

BOOKS

Felix, Rebecca. *Michael Jordan*. Minneapolis, MN: Abdo Publishing, 2022.

Flynn, Brendan. *The NBA Encyclopedia for Kids*. Minneapolis, MN: Abdo Publishing, 2022.

Mahoney, Brian. *GOATs of Basketball*. Minneapolis, MN: Abdo Publishing, 2022.

Mason, Tyler. *Michael Jordan and the Chicago Bulls*. Minneapolis, MN: Abdo Publishing, 2019.

ONLINE RESOURCES

To learn more about the Chicago Bulls, please visit **abdobooklinks.com** or scan this QR code. These links are routinely monitored and updated to provide the most current information available.

INDEX

ABOUT THE AUTHOR

Todd Kortemeier is a sportswriter and children's book author who grew up watching the Jordan Bulls dominate the NBA. He lives near Minneapolis with his wife and daughter, as well as their dog.